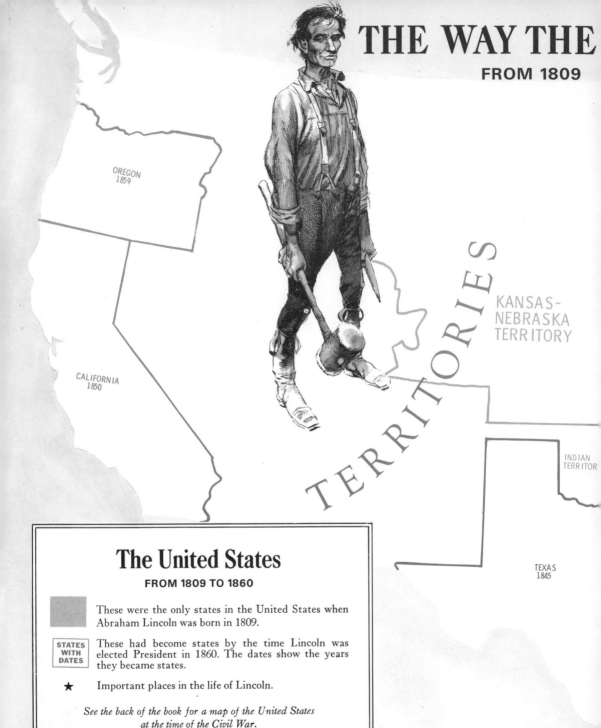

THE WAY THE

FROM 1809

OREGON
1859

KANSAS-
NEBRASKA
TERRITORY

CALIFORNIA
1850

TERRITORIES

INDIAN
TERRITOR

TEXAS
1845

The United States

FROM 1809 TO 1860

These were the only states in the United States when
Abraham Lincoln was born in 1809.

STATES WITH DATES These had become states by the time Lincoln was
elected President in 1860. The dates show the years
they became states.

★ Important places in the life of Lincoln.

*See the back of the book for a map of the United States
at the time of the Civil War.*

COUNTRY GREW

TO 1860

MINNESOTA
1858

MICHIGAN

MAINE
1820

VERMONT

NEW
HAMPSHIRE

MASSACHUSETTS

WISCONSIN
1848

MICHIGAN
1837

NEW YORK

RHODE ISLAND

CONNECTICUT

IOWA
1846

ILLINOIS
1818

INDIANA
1816

OHIO

PENNSYLVANIA

NEW
JERSEY

MARY-
LAND

DELAWARE

★ Washington, D.C.

★ New
Salem

★ Springfield

★ Vandalia

Pigeon
★ Creek

★ Knob Creek

VIRGINIA

MISSOURI
1821

OHIO

RIVER

KENTUCKY

NORTH CAROLINA

MISSISSIPPI RIVER

TENNESSEE

ARKANSAS
1836

SOUTH
CAROLINA

MISSISSIPPI
1817

ALABAMA
1819

GEORGIA

LOUISIANA
1812

★ New Orleans

FLORIDA
1845

BARBARA CARY is both a mother and an authority on Abraham
Lincoln. The first of these accomplishments stems from her marriage to
editor-author Peter Cary, and the second from a job on the *Reader's
Digest*. There she compiled a collection of Lincoln anecdotes which appeared as a book supplement. Its success led to a commission from
W. W. Norton & Company, publishers, for a full-length book on Lincoln.
She has since been actively engaged on this project, with time out to
combine her love for children and her admiration for the 16th President
in MEET ABRAHAM LINCOLN.

JACK DAVIS is not only a talented artist, he is also a busy one. His
drawings have appeared in newspapers, magazines and books, on rec-
ord jackets, subway posters, billboards and movie marquees, and they
have delighted the readers of three Step-Up Books: *Meet Abraham Lincoln, Meet The North American Indians,* and *Meet Theodore Roosevelt.*

Mr. Davis was born in Atlanta, studied at the University of Georgia
and the Art Students League, and lives now in Scarsdale, New York,
with his wife and two children.

This title was originally catalogued by the Library of Congress as follows: Cary, Barbara. Meet Abraham Lincoln. Illustrated
by Jack Davis. New York, Random House [1965] 86 p. col. illus., col. maps (on lining papers) col. ports. 22 cm. (Step-up
books). 1. Lincoln, Abraham, Pres. U.S., 1809-1865—Juvenile literature. I. Davis, Jack, Illus. II. Title. E457.905.C27   j 92
64—19131   ISBN 0-394-80057-5   ISBN 0-394-90057-X (lib. bdg.)

Meet
Abraham
Lincoln

By BARBARA CARY

Illustrated by JACK DAVIS

Step-Up Books ⌐ Random House
New York

1

Abraham Lincoln has been dead for 100 years. Yet each year, on February 12, Americans remember his birthday. He was one of the great Presidents of the United States. Americans still remember what he said. They still read what he wrote. They remember the things he did as President. They say that, if he had not lived, the United States might be two countries today instead of one.

Abraham Lincoln was born in 1809. In 1809 the United States was still a young country. Its first President, George Washington, had been dead for only ten years. In 1809 there were only 17 states.

Eight of the states were in the southern part of the country. It was warm in the South. Cotton would grow there. Some farmers had big cotton fields.

They bought Negroes to work in their fields. They made the Negroes their slaves. A slave had to do anything his owner told him to do.

Nine of the states were in the North. It was cold in the North.

It was too cold to grow cotton. So people in the North did not own slaves. They did not need them. And they did not want them. They made laws against owning slaves.

In 1809 most of the land owned by the United States was still wild. But people were moving to this wild land. They were building new homes. And they were starting new states.

When Lincoln became President, there were 34 states. In 19 of them there were laws against slavery. In 15 states people could own slaves.

Abraham Lincoln was born in one of the slave states. It was the state of Kentucky.

2

Abraham Lincoln's father was named Thomas. His mother's name was Nancy. When Abraham was little they called him Abe.

Thomas Lincoln was a carpenter. He built log cabins for people.

The Lincolns lived in a one-room
log cabin. There was a road near
their cabin. It was one of the few
roads in Kentucky. Sometimes Abe
and his sister, Sarah, played by that
road. Sometimes Abe just stood and
watched people go by.

He saw families leaving Kentucky to start new states. He saw other families coming to live in Kentucky. Some of the white families had slaves with them. The families rode. The slaves walked.

Once Abe saw a soldier on the road. Abe had been fishing that day. He had caught a little fish. His mother had told him to be good to soldiers. He gave him the fish.

Abe used the road to go to school. His school was in a log cabin. It was called a "blab" school because the children studied out loud. The noise they made sounded like "blab-blab-blab."

Abe could not go to school very often. But somehow he learned to read and write. His mother and father could not read and write. Not many country people could in those days.

Abe did not have paper to write on. He did not even have a pencil. He held a stick over a fire until the end was black. Then he wrote with it on a wooden board.

The only book he had was a Bible. Some of the words were hard. But he figured them out. He read the Bible over and over. Finally he knew most of the stories by heart.

3

When Abe was seven the Lincolns left Kentucky. One reason they left was that another man said he owned their land. Thomas thought he owned the land. He had bought it. But the other man said he had bought it first.

Thomas did not have much money. He could not pay a lawyer to find out who was right.

Another reason the Lincolns moved was that Kentucky was a slave state. Thomas and Nancy did not like living in a state where people could own slaves.

Thomas went to another state called Indiana. In Indiana slavery was against the law. Indiana was a new state. Not many people lived there. In Indiana he could buy land from the government and be sure he owned it. And he did not have to pay for it all at once.

Thomas bought some land. It was at a place called Pigeon Creek. Then he went back to Kentucky to get his family.

It was winter when the Lincolns got to Pigeon Creek. While Thomas built a cabin, they lived in a shed made of branches. The shed was very small. And it was very cold.

There was no room in it for a fire. Nancy and Sarah had to cook over an open fire outside.

Abe was a small boy. But he had to work like a man. He helped his father chop down trees to build their cabin. He helped him dig out tree stumps to clear a place to plant a garden in the spring. Abe once said that was the hardest winter he ever spent. "Those were pretty pinching times," he said.

13

4

After the first winter, things were better for the Lincolns. They had their cabin. Thomas and Abe had planted a garden. They bought some cows and pigs.

More people were moving to Pigeon Creek. An aunt and uncle of Nancy's came from Kentucky. They were Mr. and Mrs. Sparrow. The Lincolns were not as lonely as they had been.

At night the Sparrows often came to visit with the Lincolns. Abe loved to hear the grownups talk.

When Abe could not understand their talk, he asked questions. His father said he asked too many questions. But Abe said he had to ask them. "There are so many things I want to know," he said.

Sometimes the grownups told stories. Thomas told stories about his childhood in Kentucky. When Thomas was a child, his father had been killed by Indians in Kentucky. This was a scary story. But Abe liked to hear about his grandfather and the Indians.

Sometimes Abe told stories, too. They were funny ones that he made up. They made everyone laugh.

The Lincolns and the Sparrows had good times together. But the good times did not last. One fall a sickness came to Pigeon Creek. It was called "milk-sick." It came from drinking the milk of sick cows. Some of the Pigeon Creek people died from "milk-sick." Mr. and Mrs. Sparrow died from it.

Then Abe's mother got the "milk-sick." Thomas and Abe and Sarah took good care of her. They did all they could. But on a beautiful October morning, Nancy Lincoln died.

5

Abe and Sarah missed their mother badly. Thomas Lincoln missed her, too. He hardly spoke. He never smiled. Sarah tried to cook and keep house. It was hard. She was only a little girl. Sometimes she sat by the cabin door and cried.

Abe hated to see Sarah cry. He tried to cheer her up. One day he brought her a baby raccoon to play with.

"He is nice," Sarah said. "But he is not the same as a mother."

Abe knew Sarah was right.

Nothing was the same without their mother.

For more than a year, Thomas Lincoln and Abe and Sarah were sad and lonely. Then Thomas married again.

The new Mrs. Lincoln was a kind woman. She was a good wife to Thomas. She was a good mother to Abe and Sarah.

Abe loved his new mother. And she loved him. She said she could not have loved him more if he had been her own son.

A year after Thomas and Mrs. Lincoln were married, a school opened in Pigeon Creek. Mrs. Lincoln asked Thomas to send Abe to the school.

Abe was 11 years old. He was happy to go to school again. But he could not go as much as he wanted. He went for a few weeks. Then he stopped. Then he went for a few more weeks. Then he had to stop again. All the weeks added together came to less than a year. When he was grown up, Lincoln said, "I went to school by littles."

6

Sometimes Abe had to stop school to help his father on the farm. Sometimes he stopped because Thomas needed money. In those days any money a boy earned before he was 21 belonged to his father. Farmers paid Thomas 25 cents a day to have Abe work for them.

Abe worked hard. But he did not want to be a farmer. "My father taught me to farm," he once said. "But he never taught me to love it."

Abe did not like to farm. He liked to read. He began to borrow books. There were not many books in Pigeon Creek to borrow. But he borrowed all there were.

He read books at night, by the
light of the fire. One book he read
was about George Washington. He
read how Washington had helped
the United States become a new
country. Washington became a
great hero to Abe.

Another book Abe read was a book
of Indiana laws. It was not a very
exciting book. But Abe liked it.

He learned there were many laws. He wondered if a lawyer had to remember them all.

When Abe read he seemed to be in another world. He did not even hear people speak to him. It made his father cross. Thomas did not understand why Abe wanted to read. Thomas said it was enough for a boy to work hard and be strong. He said Abe was wasting his time.

Mrs. Lincoln understood Abe better. She told Thomas to let him read. She said she thought Abe would be a great man someday.

"A great lazybones, if you ask me," Thomas said.

7

By the time Abe was 19, he was
six feet four inches tall. He was
the tallest boy in Pigeon Creek.
He was the strongest boy, too.

One day a farmer told Abe he had a job for a strong boy. His son, Allen, was taking some things to New Orleans to sell. He asked Abe to go along.

Abe was excited. New Orleans was in the state of Louisiana. It was a southern city. It was 1,000 miles from Pigeon Creek!

Abe said he would like to go to New Orleans. But he would have to ask his father.

The farmer said he would pay Thomas eight dollars for each month Abe was away. That was more money than Abe had ever earned. Thomas said he could go.

Abe and Allen took the farmer's things to the Ohio River. They loaded the things on a flatboat. Then they floated down the Ohio into the great Mississippi River.

New Orleans is at the very end of the Mississippi River. It took a long time to get there.

Abe had never been to a big city before. There were houses made of brick and stone. At first he thought New Orleans was a wonderful place. But then he saw a market where slaves were being sold. Abe did not like what he saw. And he was not unhappy when he and Allen had to start back to Pigeon Creek.

8

The year after Abe got back from
New Orleans, Thomas Lincoln
wanted to move again. He had heard
the land was better in the state of
Illinois. Abe helped his father
move to Illinois. He helped him
build a cabin to live in.

Then Abe said good-bye to his family. He was 21 now. And he could work for himself.

For a year he wandered about doing odd jobs. Then he went to live in a little town called New Salem.

New Salem was a pretty town. It was near a river. Abe lived there for six years. While he was there he had many jobs.

He worked in a store. The New Salem people said he was the most honest storekeeper they had ever had. But the store failed. There was a mill in New Salem. Abe worked at the mill. He ground corn into flour. He worked as a surveyor, making maps of people's land. For a while he was the New Salem mail man.

There was no post office in the town. When the mail came, Abe put the letters in his hat. Then he carried them to people.

When people in New Salem were asked where their post office was, they always said, "Our post office is in Abe's hat."

Abe made good friends in New Salem. Everyone liked him. Ladies liked him because he was so kind and helpful. If a woman needed water from the river, Abe got it for her. If a woman needed wood for a fire, he chopped it. He even helped the mothers with their children.

He brought the children candy. He played with them. He rocked the babies to sleep. One mother said, "Abe Lincoln will do anything to help anyone."

9

The New Salem men liked Abe
because he could tell funny stories.
They liked him because he was good
at sports and games. He could jump
higher and run faster and throw a
ball farther than any of them. They
liked to talk to him, too. They liked
to talk to him about politics.

Once a week a newspaper came to New Salem. Abe learned about politics from the newspaper. He read what was being done in the Illinois state government. Then he told the New Salem men what he thought should be done. The men liked Abe's ideas. They said he should go into politics. Abe Lincoln liked the idea of going into politics.

In March, 1832, he said that he would like to be an Illinois state representative. As a representative he could help make the laws of the state. The people choose their representatives by voting. They vote for the men they like best.

The next election would be in August. Abe knew that all of his friends in New Salem would vote for him. But he knew he needed more votes than that. He would have to talk to people in other towns. If they liked what he said, he would get the votes he needed.

But Abe did not have time to go to the other towns. A war started in Illinois. And Lincoln went to fight in it.

10

The war was against some Indians in the north part of Illinois. The Indians were led by Chief Black Hawk. He said the Illinois people had taken some Indian land. Abe joined the Illinois army.

Some other young men from New
Salem joined, too. The New Salem
men asked Abe to be their captain.

It was spring when Captain Abe
and his men marched off to the war.

It rained every day. The men were wet and cold. The roads were muddy. The food for the army was in wagons. The wagons got stuck in the mud. The army had to leave the wagons behind.

Then the men had to hunt for their own food. Once Abe's men did not find any food for two days.

At last they caught an old hen. They cooked it over an open fire.

11

Abe now went back to politics. But there were only two weeks before the election. Abe could not get enough votes. There was not enough time. He lost the election.

But after two years there was another election. This time, Abe had time to work for votes. He went to many other towns. He talked to many people.

He talked to them about roads. The roads in Illinois were very bad.

Abe said that, if he was elected representative, he would vote for better roads. There were no public schools in Illinois. Abe said every child should have a chance to go to school. He said he would vote for public schools.

People liked what Abe said. In 1834 he was elected as one of the Illinois state representatives.

After Abe was elected, he was an important man. People began to call him Lincoln. Or Mr. Lincoln.

Mr. Lincoln had to go to the state capital to do his work as a representative. The capital of Illinois was called Vandalia.

Lincoln met representatives from all parts of the state in Vandalia. He found that many of them were lawyers. Lincoln had always wanted to be a lawyer. Now he had a chance. One of the representatives said he would help Lincoln become a lawyer. He gave him law books to read.

The representatives worked in Vandalia for a few weeks each year. Then they went home. Lincoln went home to New Salem. He took the law books with him. He studied very hard. He studied so hard that he taught himself to be a lawyer in a few months. He was a good lawyer. And people trusted him.

They knew he would work hard to win a law case he thought was right. He would not take a law case he thought was wrong.

Once a man in the wrong asked Lincoln to take his case. Lincoln said no. He said, "All the time I was talking to the jury, I'd be thinking I was a liar. And I believe I'd forget myself and say it out loud."

Lincoln worked hard as a state representative, too. One thing he worked to do was change the capital of Illinois. Vandalia was a small town. North of Vandalia there was a bigger town called Springfield.

Lincoln felt that it would make a much better state capital.

Some of the representatives did not want the capital moved. The representatives voted. And Lincoln's side won! Springfield became the new capital. Now Lincoln left New Salem for good. He went to live in Springfield. There was more work for a lawyer in the new capital. He opened a law office. It soon became a busy place.

One night Lincoln went to a party in Springfield. At the party he met a young lady named Mary Todd. He thought she was the prettiest young lady he had ever seen.

Abraham Lincoln asked Mary Todd to dance with him.

"Miss Todd," he said, "I want to dance with you in the worst way."

Mary Todd danced with Lincoln. Then she said, "Mr. Lincoln danced just the way he said he would. He danced in the worst way."

But Mary Todd did not really care how Lincoln danced. She liked him. When he asked her to marry him, she said "Yes."

12

Mr. and Mrs. Lincoln bought a nice house in Springfield. Sometimes Mrs. Lincoln scolded her husband about the way he behaved in the house. Mr. Lincoln liked to lie down on the floor when he read. He liked to take off his coat and tie at home. He also liked to walk around with his shoes off. He said this gave his feet a chance to breathe.

Mrs. Lincoln told Mr. Lincoln to sit up in a chair when he read. She told him to keep his coat and tie on. She said his feet did not need to breathe. They needed to have shoes on them.

She scolded him. But she loved him. "Mr. Lincoln's heart is as big as his arms are long," she said.

The Lincolns had four sons. One of them died when he was a baby. His name was Edward. The other sons were Robert and William and Thomas. Friends called them Bob and Willie and Tad. Mr. Lincoln called Thomas "Tad" because he moved as quickly as a tadpole.

Mr. Lincoln loved to play with his boys. When they were little, he carried them around on his shoulders. Sometimes he pretended to be a horse. He took them for rides in a little red wagon.

When they were older, Mr. Lincoln played ball and many other games with them. Sometimes they came to his office. While he worked, they climbed all over him. They played with his books. They used his pens for darts. They were often quite naughty. But Mr. Lincoln never thought so. He thought his boys were wonderful.

13

Abraham Lincoln was an Illinois state representative for eight years. But he wanted to do more in politics. In 1847 he got his wish. The people of his district elected him to represent them in the United States Congress.

Every district in every state sends a representative to Congress. These men meet in Washington, D. C.

When Lincoln went to Washington there were 28 states in the United States.

In 14 states it was against the law to own slaves. But in the 14 Southern states people could own slaves. And they did.

There was a slave market in Washington. Lincoln was against anyone owning slaves anywhere. Congress could not change state laws about slavery. But Washington, D. C., was not a state. It was the capital of the United States. Congress could make a law against having slavery in the capital. Lincoln thought it should. But he could not get Congress to do it.

While Lincoln was in Congress, America was at war with Mexico.

Lincoln thought the United States had started the war to get some land. And he said so. The people in Lincoln's district in Illinois did not like his saying this. They wanted the United States to have all the land it could get. They did not want Lincoln as their representative any more.

Congressmen are elected for two years. At the end of two years Lincoln went back to Springfield. For the next five years he had no political job. He worked as a lawyer. But in 1854 something happened that brought Lincoln back into politics.

14

The United States owned some land called the Kansas-Nebraska Territory. In 1820 Congress had made a law saying no one could own slaves there. But in 1854 Congress made a new law. It said this territory could have slavery if the people there voted for it. The new law made Lincoln very angry.

Lincoln said it was wrong for Congress to help slavery spread all over the United States. It was bad enough having it in the Southern states. He began making speeches against the Kansas-Nebraska law.

Another Illinois man began making speeches for the law. His name was Stephen Douglas.

Mr. Douglas was a senator. Lincoln had represented only one district in Congress. As a senator, Douglas represented everyone in the state.

In 1858 Lincoln ran for senator against Douglas. Before the election they had seven debates. First one talked. Then the other. Thousands of people came to hear their speeches. They came in trains. And in wagons. And on foot.

Douglas said he did not think slavery was wrong.

He said he did not care if there was slavery in the Kansas-Nebraska Territory. "Let the people vote on it," Stephen Douglas said.

Lincoln said that people should not be allowed to vote on things that were wrong.

Lincoln said they did not vote on stealing. Or killing. Or other wrong things. "And slavery is wrong," he said.

Douglas was a small man. People called him the "Little Giant." They called Lincoln the "Big Giant." They said the debates were a battle of the giants. They called them the "Great Debates."

15

Lincoln did not win the election for senator. Douglas did. But the Great Debates made Lincoln famous.

People all over the country talked about his speeches. Some people said Lincoln should run for President of the United States.

In 1860 there was an election for President. Lincoln and Douglas ran. So did two other men.

This time it was Abraham Lincoln who won on Election Day.

Lincoln's friends in Springfield were very happy. But Lincoln was serious, and a little sad.

Lincoln knew it would be hard to be President. The people of the North and South were angry at each other over slavery. The people in the South were angry at him, too. They knew he was against slavery. Not one Southern state had voted for him for President.

Lincoln was elected President on November 6, 1860. But he would not become President until March 4, 1861.

Between November and March, seven states in the South broke away from the United States. They did not want Lincoln as their President.

These seven states started their own country. They called it the Confederate States of America. They elected their own President. His name was Jefferson Davis.

They started a Confederate army.

The Confederate army began to take over the forts in the South. These forts belonged to the United States. But the Confederate States said the forts were on their land. And that they belonged to the Confederate States.

16

The day Lincoln became President
he made a speech. He said both the
country and the states would die
without one another. He said the
Confederate States were still part
of the United States.

He said the South must give back
the forts they had taken. But the
Confederate States did not listen.
They took still another fort. It was
Fort Sumter in South Carolina.

Lincoln asked men to join the United States Army. This call for an army made four more Southern states angry. They broke away from the United States. There were now 11 states in the Confederacy. They were all slave states.

But four other slave states did not join the Confederacy. They believed, as Lincoln did, that the states should stay united.

The country was divided. Two great armies marched against one another. And the war began.

One side was fighting to keep the states united. The other was fighting to have its own country.

The men who fought to keep the United States together called themselves Union men. They called the war a civil war. A civil war is fought between people of the same country.

The men of the South said they did not belong to the United States. They had their own country now. They said it was not a civil war. It was a war between the states.

It did not matter what it was called. Thousands and thousands of men were killed. During the war, Lincoln was always sad. Once he said, "I do not think I will ever be glad again."

17

Soon the Union army was bigger
than the Confederate army. And it
had more guns. The people of the
Union states were sure they would
win the war in no time.

Their large army marched into the South. But the Confederacy had great generals. And in the first big battle of the war the Confederate army won a great victory. It was a terrible day for the Union.

Some Northern men wanted to give up the war. Now they saw it could be a long war. No one hated the war more than Lincoln. He hated to have soldiers die. But Lincoln said the Union army must go on fighting. It must fight until the "United States" were once again united.

Lincoln saved all the soldiers' lives he could. Sometimes soldiers were shot for breaking army rules. Lincoln saved hundreds of these men from being shot.

"I always sleep better when I know I have saved some poor soldier's life," he said.

The soldiers loved Lincoln. They called him Father Abraham. And he loved them. When he met a soldier on the street he took off his hat and bowed. He went to see soldiers who were in hospitals. He stopped by every bed. He talked to every soldier. He sent letters to the families of soldiers who died. He told them how sorry he was.

Mr. Lincoln knew how the families felt. While he was President, his own son Willie died.

18

As President, Lincoln had many problems. The Union generals were losing battle after battle. He had to find better generals. Another of his problems was what to do about slavery. Many men in the North were saying Lincoln should free the slaves. Lincoln wanted to.

But the Union army needed all the help it could get. Four slave states had stayed in the Union. If the slaves were freed, these states might join the Confederacy.

But something had to be done. Slavery had caused the war. Lincoln knew there could never be peace if the country was half slave and half free. He wrote a paper called the Emancipation Proclamation. This paper said that all the slaves in the Confederacy were free.

The Emancipation Proclamation did not put an end to slavery. The Confederacy went on fighting to keep its slaves. The slaves in the Union were still not free. But it gave a new meaning to the war. Now people felt that the war was not only to keep the states united. It was also a war for freedom.

In November, 1863, Lincoln gave a speech. In this speech he put both of these meanings together.

Lincoln gave the speech at Gettysburg, Pennsylvania. There had been a great battle at Gettysburg. The soldiers who died in the battle were buried there.

Lincoln spoke for less than three minutes. He said that the United States was a country of liberty. In it all men were equal. And he said that the soldiers had died so that the United States might live.

It is one of the most beautiful speeches ever made. We call it the Gettysburg Address.

19

The Civil War lasted for four years. For two years the Union lost most of the battles. But, at last, Lincoln found generals who could win battles. One of the generals was Ulysses S. Grant. Lincoln made him the head of the army. Grant did not look much like a general.

He wore old clothes. He smoked big black cigars. But he knew how to fight.

Under General Grant the Union men began to win battles. Now Lincoln knew he could do something more about freeing the slaves.

If the Union won the war, the Emancipation Proclamation would free the slaves in the Confederate states. But Lincoln wanted to free all the slaves. And he wanted to keep the people of the United States from ever owning slaves again. He wanted this to be a law for the whole country.

To make it a law in every state Congress would have to vote for it first. Then the states would have to vote for it, too.

In January, 1865, Congress voted for this law. Then the states began to vote. Lincoln hoped they would vote for the law he wanted.

In April, General Grant's army captured the city of Richmond. Richmond was the capital of the Confederacy. The next day Lincoln walked around the city. He saw the people who had been fighting him for so long. They watched him walk by. No one made a sound.

The Confederate army was small now. The men were hungry. They did not have enough clothes. They did not have enough guns. The Confederates knew they had lost. On April 9, General Robert E. Lee, the head of the Confederate army, surrendered to General Grant. The Civil War was over.

20

The month of April, 1865, was a beautiful month in Washington. There were flowers in the gardens. There were new leaves on the trees.

At last President Lincoln could be happy again. The long, hard war was over. One by one the states were voting to free the slaves. There would soon be no more slavery in the United States. And all the states would soon be united again.

On the morning of April 14, General Grant came to call at the White House. He said how well the President looked.

In the afternoon Mr. Lincoln played with his little son Tad. And he talked to his son Bob. Bob was just home from the army. Mr. Lincoln was glad to see his soldier son.

Then the President went for a ride with Mrs. Lincoln. She said he was happy that afternoon.

That night they went to a theater to see a play. It was a funny play. Mr. Lincoln laughed a lot. He was having a good time.

Suddenly, there was a shot. At first the people in the theater thought it was part of the play.

But it was not. President Lincoln had been shot by a man who loved the Confederacy. Early the next morning President Lincoln died.

A train carried Mr. Lincoln back to Springfield. In town after town people stood to watch it go by. They could not believe their good and kind President was dead.

They knew he had loved them. And that he had loved his country, too. To keep his country united he had taken it through a long and horrible war. And because of that war it had become a country where all men were free.

Today Americans still honor and love Abraham Lincoln for what he did 100 years ago.

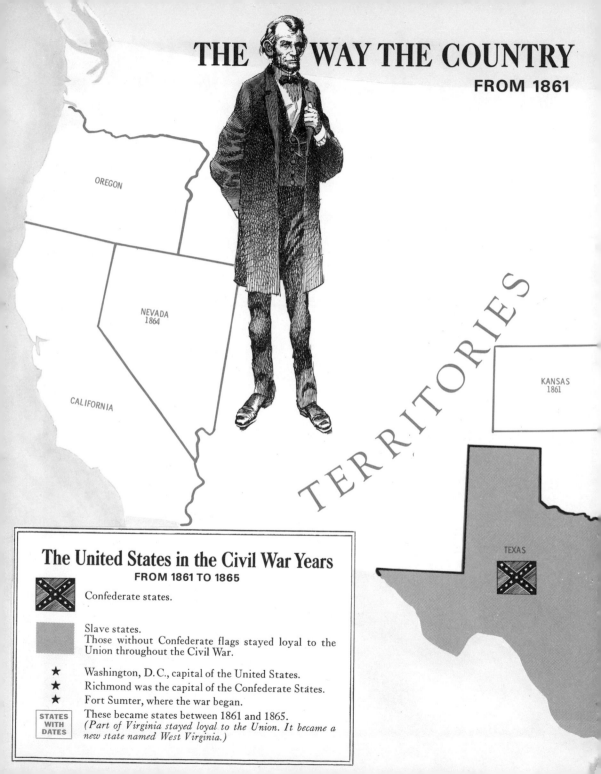

THE WAY THE COUNTRY

FROM 1861

OREGON

NEVADA
1864

CALIFORNIA

TERRITORIES

KANSAS
1861

TEXAS

The United States in the Civil War Years
FROM 1861 TO 1865

Confederate states.

Slave states.
Those without Confederate flags stayed loyal to the
Union throughout the Civil War.

★ Washington, D.C., capital of the United States.
★ Richmond was the capital of the Confederate States.
★ Fort Sumter, where the war began.

STATES WITH DATES These became states between 1861 and 1865.
*(Part of Virginia stayed loyal to the Union. It became a
new state named West Virginia.)*